Learn SAP SD (Sales and Distribution)

1. Introduction to SAP SD

1.1 Overview of SAP SD

SAP SD (Sales and Distribution) is a module of the SAP ERP (Enterprise Resource Planning) system that manages the sales and distribution processes of a company. SAP SD is designed to streamline and automate the sales and distribution processes, from the initial order creation to delivery and billing. In this article, we will provide an overview of SAP SD, its key features, and benefits.

Key Features of SAP SD

The following are some of the key features of SAP SD:

Sales Order Processing - SAP SD allows companies to manage the entire sales order process, from order creation to delivery and billing. This includes order entry, order confirmation, delivery creation, billing, and credit management.

Master Data Management - SAP SD allows companies to manage customer and material master data, which is essential for sales order processing. The master data includes information such as customer and material information, pricing, and tax information.

Logistics Execution - SAP SD integrates with other SAP modules, such as Materials Management (MM) and Production Planning (PP), to manage logistics execution. This includes shipping point determination, route determination, transportation management, and shipping scheduling.

Pricing and Discounts - SAP SD allows companies to manage pricing and discounts for products and services. This includes setting up pricing procedures, managing discounts, and managing surcharges.

Integration with Other Modules - SAP SD integrates with other SAP modules, including Materials Management (MM), Finance and Controlling (FICO), and Production Planning (PP), to streamline the sales and distribution processes and optimize the overall supply chain.

Benefits of SAP SD

The following are some of the benefits of SAP SD:

Improved Efficiency - SAP SD streamlines and automates the sales and distribution processes, which leads to improved efficiency and reduced manual intervention.

Enhanced Visibility - SAP SD provides real-time visibility into the sales and distribution processes, which enables companies to make informed decisions and respond to changes in the market quickly.

Better Resource Management - SAP SD allows companies to optimize their resources, including inventory, production capacity, and transportation, to reduce costs and improve profitability.

Improved Customer Satisfaction - SAP SD enables companies to provide a seamless customer experience, from order creation to delivery and billing, which leads to improved customer satisfaction.

Compliance - SAP SD helps companies comply with regulatory requirements, such as tax regulations, by providing accurate and timely tax information.

Conclusion

SAP SD is a module of the SAP ERP system that manages the sales and distribution processes of a company. The module includes features such as sales order processing, master data management, logistics execution, pricing and discounts, and integration with other SAP modules. The benefits of using SAP SD include improved efficiency, enhanced visibility, better resource management, improved customer satisfaction, and compliance. By implementing SAP SD, companies can optimize their sales and distribution processes, reduce costs, and improve profitability.

1.2 Benefits of using SAP SD

SAP SD (Sales and Distribution) is a module of the SAP ERP (Enterprise Resource Planning) system that helps businesses manage their sales and distribution processes. SAP SD enables companies to streamline and automate their sales processes, from the initial order creation to delivery and billing, which leads to several benefits for businesses. In this article, we will discuss the benefits of using SAP SD for businesses.

Improved Efficiency

One of the primary benefits of using SAP SD is improved efficiency. SAP SD helps businesses streamline and automate their sales and distribution processes, which reduces manual intervention and eliminates redundant tasks. For instance, SAP SD can automate order processing, billing, and inventory management, which helps to reduce the workload of the sales team and improves overall efficiency. This, in turn, helps businesses save time and resources, allowing them to focus on other important tasks, such as growing their customer base and expanding their operations.

Enhanced Visibility

SAP SD provides businesses with real-time visibility into their sales and distribution processes, which helps them make informed decisions and respond to changes in the market quickly. For example, businesses can use SAP SD to monitor sales trends, track inventory levels, and identify areas where they need to improve their operations. This information enables businesses to react quickly to changing market conditions and adjust their strategies accordingly. By having access to accurate and timely information, businesses can also improve their forecasting and planning, which leads to better decision-making and improved profitability.

Better Resource Management

SAP SD enables businesses to optimize their resources, including inventory, production capacity, and transportation, to reduce costs and improve profitability. For example, businesses can use SAP SD to manage inventory levels, track production schedules, and optimize transportation routes to reduce costs and improve delivery times. This helps businesses manage their resources more efficiently, which can result in cost savings and improved profitability.

Improved Customer Satisfaction

SAP SD enables businesses to provide a seamless customer experience, from order creation to delivery and billing, which leads to improved customer satisfaction. For example, businesses can use SAP SD to provide customers with accurate and timely information about their orders, track the status of their shipments, and provide them with real-time updates on their orders. This information helps businesses improve customer satisfaction, which can lead to increased customer loyalty and repeat business.

Compliance

SAP SD helps businesses comply with regulatory requirements, such as tax regulations, by providing accurate and timely tax information. For example, businesses can use SAP SD to manage tax codes, calculate taxes, and provide accurate tax information to their customers. This helps businesses ensure that they are complying with regulatory requirements and avoid penalties for non-compliance.

Conclusion

SAP SD is a powerful tool that helps businesses streamline and automate their sales and distribution processes. The benefits of using SAP SD include improved efficiency, enhanced visibility, better resource management, improved customer satisfaction, and compliance with regulatory requirements. By implementing SAP SD, businesses can optimize their sales and distribution processes, reduce costs, and improve profitability.

1.3 Key functionalities of SAP SD

SAP SD (Sales and Distribution) is a module of the SAP ERP (Enterprise Resource Planning) system that manages the sales and distribution processes of a company. SAP SD includes a wide range of functionalities that enable businesses to streamline and automate their sales processes, from the initial order creation to delivery and billing. In this article, we will discuss the key functionalities of SAP SD and how they help businesses improve their sales processes.

Sales Order Management

One of the core functionalities of SAP SD is sales order management. SAP SD allows businesses to create and manage sales orders, track order status, and generate order confirmations. The module provides businesses with real-time information about their sales orders, including order quantities, delivery dates, and pricing information. This helps businesses manage their sales orders more efficiently, which can lead to improved customer satisfaction.

Master Data Management

SAP SD enables businesses to manage their master data, which includes customer and material master data. This data is essential for sales order processing, and SAP SD allows businesses to manage this data more efficiently. The module provides businesses with a central repository for storing and managing customer and material data, which can be accessed by other SAP modules. This ensures that the data is consistent across the organization and reduces the likelihood of errors.

Logistics Execution

SAP SD integrates with other SAP modules, such as Materials Management (MM) and Production Planning (PP), to manage logistics execution. This includes shipping point determination, route determination, transportation management, and shipping scheduling. By integrating with other modules, SAP SD enables businesses to optimize their logistics processes, which can lead to improved efficiency and reduced costs.

Pricing and Discounts

SAP SD allows businesses to manage pricing and discounts for their products and services. The module provides businesses with a wide range of pricing options, including customer-specific pricing, volume discounts, and promotional discounts. This helps businesses improve their pricing strategies and manage their margins more effectively.

Credit Management

SAP SD includes credit management functionality that allows businesses to manage credit limits and credit exposure. This helps businesses reduce the risk of non-payment and improve their cash flow. The credit management functionality in SAP SD allows businesses to define credit limits for customers, monitor credit usage, and block orders that exceed credit limits.

Billing and Invoicing

SAP SD enables businesses to create and manage invoices for their customers. The module allows businesses to generate invoices based on sales orders, delivery notes, and billing documents. This helps businesses manage their invoicing processes more efficiently, which can improve cash flow and reduce errors.

Conclusion

SAP SD is a powerful module of the SAP ERP system that enables businesses to streamline and automate their sales processes. The key functionalities of SAP SD include sales order management, master data management, logistics execution, pricing and discounts, credit management, and billing and invoicing. By using these functionalities, businesses can improve their sales processes, reduce costs, and improve customer satisfaction. SAP SD is a valuable tool for businesses that want to optimize their sales and distribution processes and improve their overall profitability.

2. Sales Order Processing

2.1 Creating sales orders

Creating sales orders is one of the core functionalities of the SAP SD (Sales and Distribution) module. A sales order is a document that contains the details of a customer's request for a product or service. SAP SD enables businesses to create and manage sales orders, track order status, and generate order confirmations. In this article, we will discuss how to create sales orders in SAP SD and the key steps involved in the process.

Step 1: Creating a Sales Document

The first step in creating a sales order in SAP SD is to create a sales document. A sales document is a document that contains the details of the sales order, such as the customer's name, the product or service being ordered, and the price. To create a sales document, follow these steps:

Open the SAP SD module and go to the Sales and Distribution work center.

Click on the Sales Orders tab to open the Sales Order window.

Click on the Create Sales Order button to create a new sales order.

In the Create Sales Order window, select the customer for whom you want to create the sales order.

Enter the material or product that the customer is requesting, along with any other relevant information, such as the quantity and delivery date.

Step 2: Checking Availability

Once you have created the sales document, the next step is to check availability. Availability check is a process that checks the inventory levels and delivery schedules to ensure that the requested product or service is available for delivery. To check availability, follow these steps:

Click on the Availability Check button in the Create Sales Order window.

The system will check the inventory levels and delivery schedules and provide you with a message indicating whether the product is available or not.

If the product is available, you can proceed to the next step. If the product is not available, you will need to reschedule the delivery or suggest an alternative product.

Step 3: Creating Deliveries

Once the availability check is completed, the next step is to create deliveries. A delivery is a document that contains the details of the products or services that are to be delivered to the customer. To create a delivery, follow these steps:

Click on the Create Delivery button in the Sales Order window.

In the Create Delivery window, select the sales order for which you want to create the delivery.

Enter the delivery details, such as the delivery date, shipping point, and delivery quantity.

Step 4: Billing

Once the delivery is created, the next step is to create a billing document. A billing document is a document that contains the details of the invoice that is to be sent to the customer. To create a billing document, follow these steps:

Click on the Create Billing Document button in the Delivery window.

In the Create Billing Document window, select the delivery for which you want to create the billing document.

Enter the billing details, such as the billing date, payment terms, and billing quantity.

Once the billing document is created, you can send it to the customer for payment.

Conclusion

Creating sales orders is a critical component of the SAP SD module. The process involves creating a sales document, checking availability, creating deliveries, and billing. By following these steps, businesses can streamline their sales processes and improve customer satisfaction. SAP SD is a valuable tool for businesses that want to optimize their sales and distribution processes and improve their overall profitability.

2.2 Sales order configuration

Sales order configuration is a critical aspect of the SAP SD (Sales and Distribution) module. The sales order configuration determines how the sales order process is handled, from order creation to delivery and billing. In this article, we will discuss the key components of sales order configuration and how they are configured in SAP SD.

Sales Document Types

The first step in sales order configuration is to define sales document types. A sales document type is a document that defines the different types of sales orders that a business can process. For example, a business may have different sales document types for standard orders, rush orders, or returns. In SAP SD, sales document types are defined using the transaction code VOV8.

Item Categories

The next step in sales order configuration is to define item categories. An item category is a material or service that is sold in a sales order. In SAP SD, item categories are defined using the transaction code VOV7. Each item category is assigned to a sales document type, and it contains specific information about the item, such as pricing, billing, and delivery data.

Schedule Line Categories

The third step in sales order configuration is to define schedule line categories. A schedule line category is a line item in a sales order that contains information about the delivery date and the quantity of items to be delivered. In SAP SD, schedule line categories are defined using the transaction code VOV6. Each schedule line category is assigned to an item category, and it contains information about the delivery date, the order quantity, and the delivery quantity.

Partner Functions

The fourth step in sales order configuration is to define partner functions. A partner function is a role that is assigned to a partner in a sales order. A partner can be a customer, vendor, or employee. In SAP SD, partner functions are defined using the transaction code VOPA. Examples of partner functions include sold-to party, ship-to party, and bill-to party.

Pricing

The fifth step in sales order configuration is to define pricing procedures. A pricing procedure is a set of conditions that determine the price of a material or service. In SAP SD, pricing procedures are defined using the transaction code V/08. Each pricing procedure is assigned to a sales document type and contains a list of condition types that determine the price of the material or service.

Shipping

The final step in sales order configuration is to define shipping procedures. A shipping procedure is a set of rules that determine how the material or service is shipped to the customer. In SAP SD, shipping procedures are defined using the transaction code VOHU. Each shipping procedure is assigned to a delivery type and contains information about the shipping point, route, and carrier.

Conclusion

Sales order configuration is a critical aspect of the SAP SD module. The configuration determines how the sales order process is handled, from order creation to delivery and billing. The key components of sales order configuration include sales document types, item categories, schedule line categories, partner functions, pricing, and shipping. By properly configuring these components, businesses can streamline their sales processes and improve customer satisfaction. SAP SD is a valuable tool for businesses that want to optimize their sales and distribution processes and improve their overall profitability.

2.3 Order fulfillment process

The order fulfillment process is a critical component of the SAP SD (Sales and Distribution) module. The process involves fulfilling customer orders, from order creation to delivery and billing. In this article, we will discuss the key steps involved in the order fulfillment process and how they are handled in SAP SD.

Order Creation

The first step in the order fulfillment process is order creation. A customer order can be created in several ways, including through the SAP SD module or through an external system, such as an e-commerce website. In SAP SD, orders are created using sales document types, which define the type of order being created. For example, a standard order or a rush order.

Order Processing

Once the order is created, it is processed through the SAP SD module. The order is checked for accuracy and completeness, and the system checks the availability of the products or services ordered. The availability check includes checking inventory levels and delivery schedules to ensure that the requested products or services are available for delivery.

Order Confirmation

After the order has been processed, an order confirmation is generated. The order confirmation includes details of the order, such as the customer name, delivery date, and pricing information. The order confirmation is sent to the customer to confirm the order and provide them with the details of the delivery.

Shipping and Delivery

Once the order confirmation is generated, the order is prepared for shipping and delivery. The SAP SD module provides businesses with the ability to manage logistics execution, including shipping point determination, route determination, and transportation management. The module allows businesses to optimize their logistics processes, which can lead to improved efficiency and reduced costs.

Billing and Invoicing

After the order has been delivered, billing and invoicing is the final step in the order fulfillment process. SAP SD enables businesses to create and manage invoices for their customers. The module allows businesses to generate invoices based on sales orders, delivery notes, and billing documents. This helps businesses manage their invoicing processes more efficiently, which can improve cash flow and reduce errors.

Conclusion

The order fulfillment process is a critical component of the SAP SD module. The process involves fulfilling customer orders, from order creation to delivery and billing. The key steps involved in the process include order creation, order processing, order confirmation, shipping and delivery, and billing and invoicing. By using SAP SD, businesses can streamline their order fulfillment processes and improve customer satisfaction. SAP SD is a valuable tool for businesses that want to optimize their sales and distribution processes and improve their overall profitability.

2.4 Delivery creation and processing

Delivery creation and processing is a critical component of the SAP SD (Sales and Distribution) module. The delivery process involves the creation of delivery documents, which contain details of the products or services that are to be delivered to the customer. In this article, we will discuss the key steps involved in the delivery creation and processing process in SAP SD.

Delivery Creation

The first step in the delivery creation process is to create a delivery document. A delivery document is created when the order is processed and the availability check is completed. In SAP SD, delivery documents are created using delivery types, which define the type of delivery being created. For example, a standard delivery or an express delivery.

Picking and Packing

Once the delivery document is created, the next step is to pick and pack the products or services that are to be delivered. This involves selecting the products or services from the warehouse and packing them for delivery. In SAP SD, picking and packing are managed through the warehouse management module.

Goods Issue

The next step in the delivery creation and processing process is the goods issue. The goods issue involves the transfer of goods from the warehouse to the delivery vehicle. In SAP SD, the goods issue is managed through the inventory management module. Once the goods issue is completed, the products or services are ready for delivery.

Delivery Processing

After the goods issue, the delivery processing begins. The delivery processing involves the creation of the delivery document and the updating of the order status. The delivery document contains the details of the products or services that are being delivered, such as the delivery date, the shipping point, and the carrier. In SAP SD, the delivery processing is managed through the delivery processing module.

Proof of Delivery

Once the delivery has been made, the next step is to obtain a proof of delivery. A proof of delivery is a document that verifies that the products or services were delivered to the customer. In SAP SD, the proof of delivery is managed through the billing and invoicing module. The proof of delivery is an important document for businesses, as it provides evidence that the products or services were delivered, which can be used in case of disputes or claims.

Conclusion

Delivery creation and processing is a critical component of the SAP SD module. The process involves creating delivery documents, picking and packing products or services, goods issue, delivery processing, and obtaining a proof of delivery. By using SAP SD, businesses can streamline their delivery processes and improve customer satisfaction. SAP SD is a valuable tool for businesses that want to optimize their sales and distribution processes and improve their overall profitability.

2.5 Billing and invoice processing

Billing and invoice processing is a critical component of the SAP SD (Sales and Distribution) module. The billing process involves the creation of billing documents and the management of invoices. In this article, we will discuss the key steps involved in the billing and invoice processing process in SAP SD.

Billing Document Creation

The first step in the billing and invoice processing process is the creation of a billing document. The billing document is created when the delivery is made and the goods issue is completed. In SAP SD, billing documents are created using billing types, which define the type of billing document being created. For example, a standard invoice or a pro forma invoice.

Pricing

Once the billing document is created, the next step is pricing. Pricing involves the calculation of the price of the products or services being sold. In SAP SD, pricing is managed through pricing procedures, which define the conditions that determine the price of the product or service. The pricing procedure contains a list of condition types, such as discounts or taxes, that are used to calculate the final price.

Invoice Processing

After the pricing is completed, the next step is the invoice processing. The invoice processing involves the creation of the invoice and the updating of the accounting data. In SAP SD, the invoice processing is managed through the billing and invoicing module. The invoice contains the details of the products or services that were delivered, the price of the products or services, and the payment terms.

Payment Processing

After the invoice is created, the next step is the payment processing. The payment processing involves the management of the payment from the customer. In SAP SD, the payment processing is managed through the accounting module. The accounting module contains the details of the customer's payment, such as the amount paid and the date of payment.

Credit Management

The final step in the billing and invoice processing process is the credit management. The credit management involves the management of the customer's credit limit and the management of credit risk. In SAP SD, the credit management is managed through the credit management module. The credit management module contains the details of the customer's credit limit, credit risk, and payment history.

Conclusion

Billing and invoice processing is a critical component of the SAP SD module. The process involves the creation of billing documents, pricing, invoice processing, payment processing, and credit management. By using SAP SD, businesses can streamline their billing and invoicing processes and improve customer satisfaction. SAP SD is a valuable tool for businesses that want to optimize their sales and distribution processes and improve their overall profitability.

3. Master Data Management

3.1 Customer master data management

Customer master data management is a critical component of the SAP SD (Sales and Distribution) module. The management of customer master data is important to ensure accurate and timely sales and distribution processes. In this article, we will discuss the key components of customer master data management in SAP SD.

Customer Master Record

The first component of customer master data management is the customer master record. The customer master record is a database that contains all the relevant information about a customer, such as name, address, contact information, and payment terms. In SAP SD, the customer master record is created using the transaction code XD01. The customer master record is an essential component of the sales and distribution process, as it contains the information needed to process orders, deliveries, and invoices.

Customer Hierarchies

The second component of customer master data management is customer hierarchies. Customer hierarchies are used to group customers together for reporting and analysis purposes. In SAP SD, customer hierarchies are created using the transaction code VDH1. A customer hierarchy can be used to group customers by geographic location, product line, or other criteria.

Credit Management

The third component of customer master data management is credit management. Credit management is used to manage the credit limit of customers and to prevent sales to customers with a high credit risk. In SAP SD, credit management is managed using the credit management module. The credit management module contains the credit limit, payment history, and credit risk of each customer.

Sales Data

The fourth component of customer master data management is sales data. Sales data is used to track the sales activity of customers, including the history of orders, deliveries, and invoices. In SAP SD, sales data is stored in the customer master record. The sales data is used to generate reports and analytics on customer sales activity.

Marketing Data

The fifth component of customer master data management is marketing data. Marketing data is used to manage the marketing activities of customers, including the history of marketing campaigns and the responses of customers to those campaigns. In SAP SD, marketing data is stored in the customer master record. The marketing data is used to generate reports and analytics on customer marketing activity.

Conclusion

Customer master data management is a critical component of the SAP SD module. The management of customer master data is important to ensure accurate and timely sales and distribution processes. The key components of customer master data management include the customer master record, customer hierarchies, credit management, sales data, and marketing data. By using SAP SD, businesses can streamline their customer master data management processes and improve customer satisfaction. SAP SD is a valuable tool for businesses that want to optimize their sales and distribution processes and improve their overall profitability.

3.2 Material master data management

Material master data management is a critical component of the SAP SD (Sales and Distribution) module. The management of material master data is important to ensure accurate and timely sales and distribution processes. In this article, we will discuss the key components of material master data management in SAP SD.

Material Master Record

The first component of material master data management is the material master record. The material master record is a database that contains all the relevant information about a material, such as name, description, unit of measure, and price. In SAP SD, the material master record is created using the transaction code MM01. The material master record is an essential component of the sales and distribution process, as it contains the information needed to process orders, deliveries, and invoices.

Material Types

The second component of material master data management is material types. Material types are used to group materials together for reporting and analysis purposes. In SAP SD, material types are created using the transaction code OMS2. A material type can be used to group materials by product line, product category, or other criteria.

Pricing

The third component of material master data management is pricing. Pricing involves the calculation of the price of the materials being sold. In SAP SD, pricing is managed through pricing procedures, which define the conditions that determine the price of the material. The pricing procedure contains a list of condition types, such as discounts or taxes, that are used to calculate the final price.

Inventory Management

The fourth component of material master data management is inventory management. Inventory management involves the management of inventory levels and the tracking of material movements. In SAP SD, inventory management is managed through the inventory management module. The inventory management module contains the inventory levels and the movement history of each material.

Quality Management

The fifth component of material master data management is quality management. Quality management involves the management of quality control processes and the tracking of quality issues. In SAP SD, quality management is managed through the quality management module. The quality management module contains the quality control processes and the history of quality issues for each material.

Conclusion

Material master data management is a critical component of the SAP SD module. The management of material master data is important to ensure accurate and timely sales and distribution processes. The key components of material master data management include the material master record, material types, pricing, inventory management, and quality management. By using SAP SD, businesses can streamline their material master data management processes and improve customer satisfaction. SAP SD is a valuable tool for businesses that want to optimize their sales and distribution processes and improve their overall profitability.

3.3 Pricing master data management

Pricing master data management is a critical component of the SAP SD (Sales and Distribution) module. The management of pricing master data is important to ensure accurate and timely sales and distribution processes. In this article, we will discuss the key components of pricing master data management in SAP SD.

Pricing Procedure

The first component of pricing master data management is the pricing procedure. The pricing procedure is a sequence of condition types that are used to determine the price of a product or service. In SAP SD, pricing procedures are created using the transaction code V/08. The pricing procedure determines the price of the product or service based on factors such as discounts, taxes, and surcharges.

Condition Types

The second component of pricing master data management is condition types. Condition types are used to define the individual pricing elements that make up the pricing procedure. In SAP SD, condition types are created using the transaction code V/06. Condition types can include factors such as discounts, taxes, surcharges, and freight charges.

Pricing Condition Records

The third component of pricing master data management is pricing condition records. Pricing condition records are used to maintain the pricing information for individual materials or customers. In SAP SD, pricing condition records are created using the transaction code VK11. Pricing condition records contain the pricing information for a specific material or customer, including the price, discount, and other relevant information.

Pricing Agreements

The fourth component of pricing master data management is pricing agreements. Pricing agreements are used to define the pricing terms and conditions for a specific customer or group of customers. In SAP SD, pricing agreements are created using the transaction code VBO1. Pricing agreements can include factors such as pricing discounts, volume discounts, and promotional pricing.

Price Lists

The fifth component of pricing master data management is price lists. Price lists are used to define the pricing information for a group of materials or services. In SAP SD, price lists are created using the transaction code V/08. Price lists can be used to define the pricing information for a specific product line or product category.

Conclusion

Pricing master data management is a critical component of the SAP SD module. The management of pricing master data is important to ensure accurate and timely sales and distribution processes. The key components of pricing master data management include the pricing procedure, condition types, pricing condition records, pricing agreements, and price lists. By using SAP SD, businesses can streamline their pricing master data management processes and improve customer satisfaction. SAP SD is a valuable tool for businesses that want to optimize their sales and distribution processes and improve their overall profitability.

4. Logistics Execution

4.1 Shipping point determination

Shipping point determination is a critical component of the SAP SD (Sales and Distribution) module's Logistics Execution process. The shipping point is the location from which the goods are shipped to the customer. The shipping point determination process ensures that the correct shipping point is determined based on the delivery document and the material being shipped. In this article, we will discuss the key components of shipping point determination in SAP SD.

Shipping Point

The first component of shipping point determination is the shipping point. The shipping point is the location from which the goods are shipped to the customer. In SAP SD, shipping points are defined as a combination of a plant and a storage location. The shipping point determines the shipping procedures and the transportation methods for the goods being shipped.

Delivery Document

The second component of shipping point determination is the delivery document. The delivery document is created when a delivery is created in SAP SD. The delivery document contains the details of the goods being shipped, including the material being shipped, the quantity being shipped, and the shipping address.

Shipping Conditions

The third component of shipping point determination is the shipping conditions. Shipping conditions are used to determine the appropriate shipping point based on the delivery document and the material being shipped. In SAP SD, shipping conditions are created using the transaction code OVXC. The shipping conditions include factors such as the shipping point, the delivery date, and the transportation methods.

Shipping Point Determination Procedure

The fourth component of shipping point determination is the shipping point determination procedure. The shipping point determination procedure is a set of rules that are used to determine the appropriate shipping point based on the delivery document and the material being shipped. In SAP SD, the shipping point determination procedure is defined using the transaction code OVLP. The shipping point determination procedure includes rules such as the shipping point priority, the delivery plant, and the shipping conditions.

Conclusion

Shipping point determination is a critical component of the Logistics Execution process in the SAP SD module. The shipping point is the location from which the goods are shipped to the customer, and it is important to ensure that the correct shipping point is determined based on the delivery document and the material being shipped. The key components of shipping point determination include the shipping point, the delivery document, shipping conditions, and the shipping point determination procedure. By using SAP SD, businesses can streamline their shipping point determination processes and improve customer satisfaction. SAP SD is a valuable tool for businesses that want to optimize their logistics execution processes and improve their overall profitability.

4.2 Route determination

Route determination is a critical component of the SAP SD (Sales and Distribution) module's Logistics Execution process. The route determines the transportation methods and the sequence of the delivery stops for the goods being shipped. Route determination ensures that the correct route is determined based on the shipping point and the shipping conditions. In this article, we will discuss the key components of route determination in SAP SD.

Route

The first component of route determination is the route. The route is a sequence of transportation methods and delivery stops for the goods being shipped. In SAP SD, the route is defined using the transaction code OVTR. The route determines the transportation methods and the sequence of the delivery stops.

Shipping Point

The second component of route determination is the shipping point. The shipping point is the location from which the goods are shipped to the customer. In SAP SD, the shipping point is determined based on the delivery document and the material being shipped.

Shipping Conditions

The third component of route determination is the shipping conditions. Shipping conditions are used to determine the appropriate route based on the shipping point and the shipping conditions. In SAP SD, shipping conditions are created using the transaction code OVXC. The shipping conditions include factors such as the delivery date, the shipping point, and the transportation methods.

Route Determination Procedure

The fourth component of route determination is the route determination procedure. The route determination procedure is a set of rules that are used to determine the appropriate route based on the shipping point and the shipping conditions. In SAP SD, the route determination procedure is defined using the transaction code OVLP. The route determination procedure includes rules such as the route priority, the shipping point, and the shipping conditions.

Conclusion

Route determination is a critical component of the Logistics Execution process in the SAP SD module. The route determines the transportation methods and the sequence of the delivery stops for the goods being shipped. The key components of route determination include the route, shipping point, shipping conditions, and the route determination procedure. By using SAP SD, businesses can streamline their route determination processes and improve customer satisfaction. SAP SD is a valuable tool for businesses that want to optimize their logistics execution processes and improve their overall profitability.

4.3 Shipping scheduling

Shipping scheduling is a critical component of the SAP SD (Sales and Distribution) module's Logistics Execution process. Shipping scheduling involves the coordination of transportation activities, including the planning and scheduling of shipments. In this article, we will discuss the key components of shipping scheduling in SAP SD.

Transportation Planning

The first component of shipping scheduling is transportation planning. Transportation planning involves the planning and coordination of transportation activities, including the selection of carriers and the determination of transportation routes. In SAP SD, transportation planning is managed through the Transportation Management (TM) module.

Delivery Schedule

The second component of shipping scheduling is the delivery schedule. The delivery schedule is the schedule of shipments and deliveries that need to be made to customers. In SAP SD, the delivery schedule is managed through the Sales and Distribution (SD) module.

Shipping Calendar

The third component of shipping scheduling is the shipping calendar. The shipping calendar is used to schedule the shipping of goods to customers. In SAP SD, the shipping calendar is created using the transaction code OVAB. The shipping calendar can be used to schedule shipments based on factors such as shipping days and holidays.

Delivery Priority

The fourth component of shipping scheduling is the delivery priority. The delivery priority is used to determine the order in which deliveries are made to customers. In SAP SD, the delivery priority is determined based on factors such as the customer's location and the delivery date.

Transportation Execution

The fifth component of shipping scheduling is transportation execution. Transportation execution involves the actual transportation of goods to the customer. In SAP SD, transportation execution is managed through the Transportation Management (TM) module. The TM module includes features such as shipment tracking and carrier selection.

Conclusion

Shipping scheduling is a critical component of the Logistics Execution process in the SAP SD module. The coordination of transportation activities, including the planning and scheduling of shipments, is important to ensure that goods are delivered to customers in a timely and efficient manner. The key components of shipping scheduling include transportation planning, the delivery schedule, the shipping calendar, delivery priority, and transportation execution. By using SAP SD, businesses can streamline their shipping scheduling processes and improve customer satisfaction. SAP SD is a valuable tool for businesses that want to optimize their logistics execution processes and improve their overall profitability.

4.4 Transportation management

Transportation management is a critical component of the SAP SD (Sales and Distribution) module's Logistics Execution process. Transportation management involves the planning, execution, and monitoring of transportation activities, including the selection of carriers, transportation planning, and the tracking of shipments. In this article, we will discuss the key components of transportation management in SAP SD.

Transportation Planning

The first component of transportation management is transportation planning. Transportation planning involves the selection of carriers, the determination of transportation routes, and the scheduling of shipments. In SAP SD, transportation planning is managed through the Transportation Management (TM) module. The TM module includes features such as carrier selection, route optimization, and delivery scheduling.

Shipment Execution

The second component of transportation management is shipment execution. Shipment execution involves the actual transportation of goods to the customer. In SAP SD, shipment execution is managed through the Transportation Management (TM) module. The TM module includes features such as shipment tracking and carrier performance monitoring.

Freight Cost Management

The third component of transportation management is freight cost management. Freight cost management involves the calculation and management of freight costs associated with the transportation of goods. In SAP SD, freight cost management is managed through the Transportation Management (TM) module. The TM module includes features such as freight cost calculation and cost allocation.

Transportation Analytics

The fourth component of transportation management is transportation analytics. Transportation analytics involves the monitoring and analysis of transportation activities to identify areas for improvement and optimization. In SAP SD, transportation analytics is managed through the Transportation Management (TM) module. The TM module includes features such as transportation reporting and performance monitoring.

Conclusion

Transportation management is a critical component of the Logistics Execution process in the SAP SD module. The planning, execution, and monitoring of transportation activities are important to ensure that goods are delivered to customers in a timely and efficient manner. The key components of transportation management include transportation planning, shipment execution, freight cost management, and transportation analytics. By using SAP SD, businesses can streamline their transportation management processes and improve customer satisfaction. SAP SD is a valuable tool for businesses that want to optimize their logistics execution processes and improve their overall profitability.

5. Pricing and Discounts

5.1 Pricing procedure configuration

Pricing and discounts are critical components of the SAP SD (Sales and Distribution) module, as they determine the pricing of products and services sold to customers. The pricing procedure is a sequence of condition types that are used to calculate the price of a product or service. In this article, we will discuss the key components of pricing procedure configuration in SAP SD.

Condition Types

The first component of pricing procedure configuration is the condition types. Condition types are used to define the individual pricing elements that make up the pricing procedure. In SAP SD, condition types are created using the transaction code V/06. Condition types can include factors such as discounts, taxes, surcharges, and freight charges.

Access Sequence

The second component of pricing procedure configuration is the access sequence. The access sequence is a sequence of condition tables that are used to determine the appropriate condition record for a specific condition type. In SAP SD, the access sequence is defined using the transaction code V/07.

Condition Table

The third component of pricing procedure configuration is the condition table. The condition table is a table that is used to store the pricing information for a specific condition type. In SAP SD, condition tables are defined using the transaction code V/03.

Pricing Procedure

The fourth component of pricing procedure configuration is the pricing procedure. The pricing procedure is a sequence of condition types that are used to determine the price of a product or service. In SAP SD, pricing procedures are created using the transaction code V/08. The pricing procedure determines the price of the product or service based on factors such as discounts, taxes, and surcharges.

Pricing Procedure Determination

The fifth component of pricing procedure configuration is the pricing procedure determination. The pricing procedure determination is a set of rules that are used to determine the appropriate pricing procedure for a specific customer or group of customers. In SAP SD, pricing procedure determination is managed through the Sales Area Data section of the customer master record.

Conclusion

Pricing procedure configuration is a critical component of the Pricing and Discounts process in the SAP SD module. The management of pricing master data is important to ensure accurate and timely pricing of products and services sold to customers. The key components of pricing procedure configuration include condition types, access sequence, condition table, pricing procedure, and pricing procedure determination. By using SAP SD, businesses can streamline their pricing procedure configuration processes and improve customer satisfaction. SAP SD is a valuable tool for businesses that want to optimize their sales and distribution processes and improve their overall profitability.

5.2 Discount and surcharge management

Discounts and surcharges are critical components of the SAP SD (Sales and Distribution) module's pricing and discounts process. Discounts are price reductions that are offered to customers, while surcharges are price increases. In this article, we will discuss the key components of discount and surcharge management in SAP SD.

Discounts

The first component of discount management is the discount condition type. The discount condition type is used to define the type of discount that is being offered, such as a percentage or fixed amount. In SAP SD, the discount condition type is created using the transaction code V/06.

The second component of discount management is the pricing procedure. The pricing procedure is a sequence of condition types that are used to determine the price of a product or service. In SAP SD, discounts are incorporated into the pricing procedure.

The third component of discount management is the discount condition record. The discount condition record is used to define the specific discount being offered, including the percentage or fixed amount. In SAP SD, the discount condition record is managed through the transaction code VK11.

Surcharges

The first component of surcharge management is the surcharge condition type. The surcharge condition type is used to define the type of surcharge that is being added, such as a percentage or fixed amount. In SAP SD, the surcharge condition type is created using the transaction code V/06.

The second component of surcharge management is the pricing procedure. The pricing procedure is a sequence of condition types that are used to determine the price of a product or service. In SAP SD, surcharges are incorporated into the pricing procedure.

The third component of surcharge management is the surcharge condition record. The surcharge condition record is used to define the specific surcharge being added, including the percentage or fixed amount. In SAP SD, the surcharge condition record is managed through the transaction code VK11.

Conclusion

Discount and surcharge management is a critical component of the pricing and discounts process in the SAP SD module. The management of pricing master data is important to ensure accurate and timely pricing of products and services sold to customers. The key components of discount and surcharge management include the discount and surcharge condition type, the pricing procedure, and the discount and surcharge condition record. By using SAP SD, businesses can streamline their discount and surcharge management processes and improve customer satisfaction. SAP SD is a valuable tool for businesses that want to optimize their sales and distribution processes and improve their overall profitability.

5.3 Pricing condition types and condition tables

Pricing condition types and condition tables are critical components of the SAP SD (Sales and Distribution) module's pricing and discounts process. Condition types are used to define the individual pricing elements that make up the pricing procedure, while condition tables are used to store the pricing information for a specific condition type. In this article, we will discuss the key components of pricing condition types and condition tables in SAP SD.

Pricing Condition Types

Pricing condition types are used to define the individual pricing elements that make up the pricing procedure. Pricing condition types are used to represent factors such as discounts, taxes, surcharges, and freight charges. In SAP SD, pricing condition types are created using the transaction code V/06.

There are several different types of pricing condition types, including:

Discounts: These are price reductions that are offered to customers.

Taxes: These are additional charges that are added to the price of a product or service in order to cover taxes.

Surcharges: These are price increases that are added to the price of a product or service.

Freight Charges: These are charges that are added to the price of a product or service to cover shipping and handling costs.

Pricing Condition Tables

Pricing condition tables are used to store the pricing information for a specific condition type. Pricing condition tables are used to store the condition records for each pricing condition type. In SAP SD, pricing condition tables are created using the transaction code V/03.

The pricing condition table includes the following fields:

Condition Type: This field specifies the type of pricing condition being stored in the table.

Key Combination: This field specifies the combination of key fields that uniquely identify the condition record.

Condition Record: This field specifies the value of the pricing condition being stored in the table.

Scale: This field specifies the quantity or value scale that applies to the pricing condition.

Currency: This field specifies the currency that the pricing condition is being applied in.

Conclusion

Pricing condition types and condition tables are critical components of the pricing and discounts process in the SAP SD module. The management of pricing master data is important to ensure accurate and timely pricing of products and services sold to customers. The key components of pricing condition types and condition tables include the pricing condition types used to define the individual pricing elements that make up the pricing procedure, and the pricing condition tables used to store the pricing information for a specific condition type. By using SAP SD, businesses can streamline their pricing condition types and condition tables management processes and improve customer satisfaction. SAP SD is a valuable tool for businesses that want to optimize their sales and distribution processes and improve their overall profitability.

6. Integration with Other Modules

6.1 Integration with Materials Management (MM)

The integration of SAP SD (Sales and Distribution) module with Materials Management (MM) module is essential for an efficient and streamlined business process. The MM module is responsible for managing the procurement of materials and inventory management, while the SD module is responsible for managing the sales and distribution process. In this article, we will discuss the key components of the integration of SAP SD module with MM module.

Sales Order Processing and Material Availability Check

The first component of the integration is the sales order processing and material availability check. When a sales order is created in the SAP SD module, it checks for the availability of the materials in the inventory managed by the MM module. If the materials are not available, a purchase requisition is automatically created in the MM module. This ensures that materials are procured in a timely manner and customer orders are fulfilled efficiently.

Delivery Processing and Inventory Management

The second component of the integration is the delivery processing and inventory management. When a delivery is created in the SAP SD module, the inventory levels in the MM module are updated. This ensures that the inventory levels are accurate and up-to-date, and that the materials are available for future sales orders.

Invoicing and Material Valuation

The third component of the integration is the invoicing and material valuation. When an invoice is created in the SAP SD module, the corresponding inventory value is updated in the MM module. This ensures that the financial records are accurate and up-to-date, and that the materials are valued correctly.

Intercompany Sales and Stock Transfers

The fourth component of the integration is intercompany sales and stock transfers. The integration between the SD and MM modules enables intercompany sales and stock transfers to be managed seamlessly. The inventory levels in the MM module are updated when stock is transferred between different company codes or plant locations, ensuring that the inventory records are accurate and up-to-date.

Conclusion

The integration of the SAP SD module with the MM module is essential for an efficient and streamlined business process. The key components of the integration include sales order processing and material availability check, delivery processing and inventory management, invoicing and material valuation, and intercompany sales and stock transfers. By using SAP SD and MM modules, businesses can optimize their sales and distribution processes and inventory management processes, ensuring that customer orders are fulfilled efficiently and inventory levels are accurate and up-to-date.

6.2 Integration with Finance and Controlling (FICO)

The integration of SAP SD (Sales and Distribution) module with Finance and Controlling (FICO) module is essential for a business to manage their financial operations and sales processes. The FICO module manages financial accounting, cost accounting, and internal orders, while the SD module manages sales orders, deliveries, and invoicing. In this article, we will discuss the key components of the integration of SAP SD module with FICO module.

Sales Order Processing and Account Determination

The first component of the integration is the sales order processing and account determination. When a sales order is created in the SAP SD module, the account determination is automatically triggered in the FICO module. The account determination process determines the appropriate G/L (General Ledger) accounts that should be debited and credited for the transaction.

Delivery Processing and Material Valuation

The second component of the integration is the delivery processing and material valuation. When a delivery is created in the SAP SD module, the material valuation is updated in the FICO module. The material valuation process determines the value of the inventory that is being shipped, and updates the corresponding inventory accounts in the FICO module.

Invoicing and Accounts Receivable Management

The third component of the integration is the invoicing and accounts receivable management. When an invoice is created in the SAP SD module, the corresponding accounts receivable account is updated in the FICO module. This ensures that the financial records are accurate and up-to-date, and that the accounts receivable are being managed effectively.

Credit Management and Accounts Payable Management

The fourth component of the integration is the credit management and accounts payable management. The integration between the SD and FICO modules enables credit management to be managed effectively, ensuring that customer credit limits are being monitored and managed. The integration also enables accounts payable management to be managed effectively, ensuring that vendor invoices are processed and paid in a timely manner.

Conclusion

The integration of the SAP SD module with the FICO module is essential for managing financial operations and sales processes effectively. The key components of the integration include sales order processing and account determination, delivery processing and material valuation, invoicing and accounts receivable management, and credit management and accounts payable management. By using SAP SD and FICO modules, businesses can optimize their financial operations and sales processes, ensuring that financial records are accurate and up-to-date, and that the sales processes are being managed effectively.

6.3 Integration with Production Planning (PP)

The integration of SAP SD (Sales and Distribution) module with Production Planning (PP) module is essential for managing the production processes and sales operations of a business. The PP module is responsible for creating and managing production plans, while the SD module is responsible for managing the sales and distribution process. In this article, we will discuss the key components of the integration of SAP SD module with PP module.

Sales Order Processing and Material Requirement Planning (MRP)

The first component of the integration is the sales order processing and material requirement planning (MRP). When a sales order is created in the SAP SD module, it triggers the material requirement planning process in the PP module. The MRP process determines the raw materials and components that are needed to fulfill the sales order and creates a production plan.

Delivery Processing and Production Execution

The second component of the integration is the delivery processing and production execution. When a delivery is created in the SAP SD module, it triggers the production execution process in the PP module. The production execution process generates the production orders and schedules for the production process. This ensures that the production process is aligned with the sales order fulfillment process and that production capacity is optimized.

Invoicing and Production Cost Management

The third component of the integration is the invoicing and production cost management. When an invoice is created in the SAP SD module, the corresponding production cost is updated in the PP module. The production cost management process determines the cost of producing the product or service and updates the corresponding cost accounts in the financial records.

Sales and Operations Planning (S&OP)

The fourth component of the integration is the sales and operations planning (S&OP). The integration between the SD and PP modules enables businesses to optimize their sales and production planning processes. The S&OP process aligns the sales and production plans to ensure that production capacity is optimized and sales orders are fulfilled efficiently.

Conclusion

The integration of the SAP SD module with the PP module is essential for managing the production processes and sales operations of a business. The key components of the integration include sales order processing and material requirement planning, delivery processing and production execution, invoicing and production cost management, and sales and operations planning. By using SAP SD and PP modules, businesses can optimize their production processes and sales operations, ensuring that customer orders are fulfilled efficiently and production capacity is optimized.

7. Reporting and Analytics

7.1 Key performance indicators (KPIs)

Key Performance Indicators (KPIs) are critical for evaluating the performance of business processes in any organization. In the context of the SAP SD (Sales and Distribution) module, KPIs are used to measure the effectiveness of the sales and distribution process. In this article, we will discuss the key KPIs that are used in the SAP SD module and how they can be used to improve business performance.

Order-to-Cash Cycle Time

The order-to-cash cycle time is the time it takes for a customer order to be fulfilled and paid for. This KPI measures the effectiveness of the sales and distribution process in terms of customer satisfaction, order accuracy, and speed of order fulfillment. By monitoring the order-to-cash cycle time, businesses can identify process inefficiencies and bottlenecks and take action to improve the overall performance of the sales and distribution process.

Sales Volume and Revenue

Sales volume and revenue are key KPIs that are used to measure the effectiveness of the sales and distribution process. These KPIs are important because they provide insight into the success of the sales process in terms of the quantity and value of products sold. By monitoring sales volume and revenue, businesses can identify trends and patterns in customer buying behavior and take action to improve the sales and distribution process.

Customer Satisfaction

Customer satisfaction is a critical KPI that measures the effectiveness of the sales and distribution process in terms of meeting customer needs and expectations. This KPI is important because it provides insight into the overall health of the customer relationship and the likelihood of future sales. By monitoring customer satisfaction, businesses can identify areas for improvement in the sales and distribution process and take action to improve customer satisfaction.

Order Processing Accuracy

Order processing accuracy is a key KPI that measures the effectiveness of the sales and distribution process in terms of the accuracy of customer orders. This KPI is important because it provides insight into the overall quality of the sales and distribution process and the level of trust customers have in the business. By monitoring order processing accuracy, businesses can identify process inefficiencies and take action to improve the overall accuracy of customer orders.

Conclusion

KPIs are critical for measuring the effectiveness of the sales and distribution process in the SAP SD module. The key KPIs that are used in the module include order-to-cash cycle time, sales volume and revenue, customer satisfaction, and order processing accuracy. By monitoring these KPIs, businesses can identify areas for improvement in the sales and distribution process and take action to improve the overall performance of the module. SAP SD module provides various reporting and analytics tools that can be used to track these KPIs and improve the overall business performance.

7.2 Production planning reports

Production planning reports are critical for managing the production process in any manufacturing organization. In the context of the SAP PP (Production Planning) module, reports provide insight into the production process and enable businesses to make data-driven decisions to improve production efficiency and quality. In this article, we will discuss the key production planning reports that are available in the SAP PP module and how they can be used to improve business performance.

Capacity Requirements Planning (CRP) Report

The Capacity Requirements Planning (CRP) report provides an overview of the capacity requirements for the production process. This report is used to identify production bottlenecks and ensure that the production process is aligned with the production capacity of the organization. By monitoring the CRP report, businesses can identify areas for improvement in the production process and take action to improve the overall capacity planning process.

Material Requirements Planning (MRP) Report

The Material Requirements Planning (MRP) report provides an overview of the raw materials and components that are required for the production process. This report is used to ensure that the materials are available when needed and that the production process is not delayed due to material shortages. By monitoring the MRP report, businesses can identify areas for improvement in the material procurement process and take action to improve the overall efficiency of the production process.

Shop Floor Control (SFC) Report

The Shop Floor Control (SFC) report provides an overview of the production process on the shop floor. This report is used to ensure that the production process is aligned with the production schedule and that the production process is being executed efficiently. By monitoring the SFC report, businesses can identify areas for improvement in the production process and take action to improve the overall efficiency of the production process.

Production Order Status Report

The Production Order Status report provides an overview of the status of the production orders. This report is used to ensure that the production orders are being executed efficiently and that the production process is aligned with the production schedule. By monitoring the Production Order Status report, businesses can identify areas for improvement in the production order process and take action to improve the overall efficiency of the production process.

Conclusion

Production planning reports are critical for managing the production process in the SAP PP module. The key reports that are available in the module include the Capacity Requirements Planning (CRP) report, the Material Requirements Planning (MRP) report, the Shop Floor Control (SFC) report, and the Production Order Status report. By monitoring these reports, businesses can identify areas for improvement in the production process and take action to improve the overall efficiency and quality of the production process. SAP PP module provides various reporting and analytics tools that can be used to track these reports and improve the overall business performance.

7.3 Sales and distribution reports

Sales and distribution reports are critical for managing the sales and distribution process in any organization. In the context of the SAP SD (Sales and Distribution) module, reports provide insight into the sales process and enable businesses to make data-driven decisions to improve sales efficiency and quality. In this article, we will discuss the key sales and distribution reports that are available in the SAP SD module and how they can be used to improve business performance.

Sales Order Report

The Sales Order report provides an overview of the sales orders that have been placed by customers. This report is used to track the status of the sales orders and ensure that the orders are being fulfilled efficiently. By monitoring the Sales Order report, businesses can identify areas for improvement in the sales order process and take action to improve the overall efficiency of the sales process.

Delivery Document Report

The Delivery Document report provides an overview of the deliveries that have been made to customers. This report is used to track the status of the deliveries and ensure that the deliveries are being made on time. By monitoring the Delivery Document report, businesses can identify areas for improvement in the delivery process and take action to improve the overall efficiency of the sales process.

Billing Document Report

The Billing Document report provides an overview of the invoices that have been issued to customers. This report is used to track the status of the invoices and ensure that the invoices are being issued accurately and on time. By monitoring the Billing Document report, businesses can identify areas for improvement in the invoicing process and take action to improve the overall efficiency of the sales process.

Sales Analysis Report

The Sales Analysis report provides an overview of the sales performance of the business. This report is used to track sales volume, revenue, and profit margins. By monitoring the Sales Analysis report, businesses can identify trends and patterns in customer buying behavior and take action to improve the overall sales performance of the business.

Credit Management Report

The Credit Management report provides an overview of the credit management process. This report is used to track customer credit limits, credit hold status, and credit exposure. By monitoring the Credit Management report, businesses can identify areas for improvement in the credit management process and take action to improve the overall credit management process.

Conclusion

Sales and distribution reports are critical for managing the sales and distribution process in the SAP SD module. The key reports that are available in the module include the Sales Order report, the Delivery Document report, the Billing Document report, the Sales Analysis report, and the Credit Management report. By monitoring these reports, businesses can identify areas for improvement in the sales and distribution process and take action to improve the overall efficiency and quality of the sales process. SAP SD module provides various reporting and analytics tools that can be used to track these reports and improve the overall business performance.

8. Best Practices for SAP SD Implementation

8.1 Key considerations for SAP SD implementation

Implementing the SAP SD (Sales and Distribution) module can be a complex and challenging process. It requires careful planning, coordination, and communication to ensure that the implementation is successful and meets the needs of the business. In this article, we will discuss the key considerations for SAP SD implementation and best practices for ensuring a successful implementation.

Define Business Requirements

The first step in SAP SD implementation is to define the business requirements. This involves identifying the specific needs of the business, such as sales order processing, delivery management, and invoicing. By defining the business requirements, businesses can ensure that the implementation is aligned with their needs and that the module is configured to meet their specific requirements.

Develop a Project Plan

Developing a project plan is critical for ensuring that the implementation is completed on time and within budget. This involves identifying the key milestones, timelines, and resource requirements for the project. By developing a project plan, businesses can ensure that the implementation is completed efficiently and effectively.

Configuration and Customization

The SAP SD module provides extensive configuration options to meet the specific needs of businesses. However, it is important to strike a balance between configuration and customization. Configuring the module to meet the business requirements is important, but customization should be kept to a minimum to ensure that the implementation is efficient and cost-effective.

Data Migration

Data migration is an important consideration in SAP SD implementation. It involves moving data from the existing system to the new SAP system. Data migration requires careful planning, execution, and testing to ensure that the data is accurate and complete. By ensuring data accuracy and completeness, businesses can avoid data-related issues and ensure a smooth transition to the new system.

User Training

User training is critical for ensuring that employees can effectively use the SAP SD module. Training should be provided to all employees who will be using the module, including sales representatives, customer service representatives, and finance personnel. By providing comprehensive training, businesses can ensure that the implementation is successful and that the employees are able to use the module efficiently and effectively.

Change Management

Change management is an important consideration in SAP SD implementation. The implementation may require changes to business processes, job roles, and responsibilities. By managing change effectively, businesses can ensure that the implementation is successful and that employees are able to adapt to the new system.

Conclusion

SAP SD implementation requires careful planning, coordination, and communication to ensure a successful implementation. The key considerations for implementation include defining business requirements, developing a project plan, configuring and customizing the module, data migration, user training, and change management. By following best practices and considering these key factors, businesses can ensure a successful implementation of the SAP SD module and improve their sales and distribution process.

8.2 Common challenges and how to address them

Implementing the SAP SD (Sales and Distribution) module can be a complex process, and there are a number of common challenges that businesses may face during the implementation. These challenges can range from issues with data migration to problems with user adoption. In this article, we will discuss some of the common challenges that businesses may face during SAP SD implementation and best practices for addressing them.

Data Migration Issues

Data migration is a critical aspect of SAP SD implementation, but it can also be one of the most challenging. Businesses may face issues with data accuracy, completeness, and consistency during the migration process. To address these issues, businesses should develop a comprehensive data migration plan that includes data mapping, data cleansing, and data testing. By ensuring that data is accurate and complete, businesses can avoid data-related issues and ensure a smooth transition to the new system.

Configuration Challenges

The SAP SD module provides extensive configuration options, which can be both a strength and a challenge. Businesses may face challenges with configuring the module to meet their specific requirements. To address these challenges, businesses should work closely with their SAP implementation team to identify the most appropriate configuration options for their business. It is important to balance configuration and customization to ensure that the implementation is efficient and cost-effective.

User Adoption Issues

User adoption is another common challenge during SAP SD implementation. Businesses may face resistance from employees who are not familiar with the new system or who are resistant to change. To address these issues, businesses should provide comprehensive user training and develop a change management plan that includes communication, engagement, and incentives for using the new system. By promoting user adoption, businesses can ensure that the implementation is successful and that the module is being used efficiently and effectively.

Integration Challenges

SAP SD is an integral part of the overall SAP ecosystem, and businesses may face challenges with integrating the module with other SAP modules or third-party systems. To address these challenges, businesses should work closely with their SAP implementation team to identify the most appropriate integration options for their business. It is important to ensure that the integration is seamless and that data is being transferred accurately and efficiently between systems.

Testing Issues

Testing is an important aspect of SAP SD implementation, but it can also be one of the most challenging. Businesses may face issues with testing, such as inadequate testing or insufficient testing resources. To address these issues, businesses should develop a comprehensive testing plan that includes unit testing, integration testing, and user acceptance testing. By ensuring that testing is comprehensive and effective, businesses can avoid issues and ensure a successful implementation.

Conclusion

Implementing the SAP SD module can be a complex process, and businesses may face a number of common challenges during the implementation. These challenges can include issues with data migration, configuration, user adoption, integration, and testing. By following best practices and addressing these challenges proactively, businesses can ensure a successful implementation of the SAP SD module and improve their sales and distribution process.

8.3 Tips for successful SAP SD implementation

Implementing the SAP SD (Sales and Distribution) module is a significant undertaking for any business. A successful implementation requires careful planning, coordination, and communication between the business and the implementation team. In this article, we will discuss some tips for successful SAP SD implementation, based on best practices and lessons learned from previous implementations.

Define Clear Business Objectives

The first step in successful SAP SD implementation is to define clear business objectives. This involves identifying the specific needs of the business, such as sales order processing, delivery management, and invoicing. By defining clear business objectives, businesses can ensure that the implementation is aligned with their needs and that the module is configured to meet their specific requirements.

Establish a Clear Project Plan

Developing a clear project plan is critical for ensuring that the implementation is completed on time and within budget. This involves identifying the key milestones, timelines, and resource requirements for the project. By establishing a clear project plan, businesses can ensure that the implementation is completed efficiently and effectively.

Collaborate with the Implementation Team

Successful SAP SD implementation requires close collaboration between the business and the implementation team. The implementation team should be involved in the project from the beginning, and they should work closely with the business to ensure that the implementation is aligned with their needs. By collaborating with the implementation team, businesses can ensure that the module is configured correctly and that the implementation is successful.

Conduct Comprehensive User Training

Comprehensive user training is critical for ensuring that employees can effectively use the SAP SD module. Training should be provided to all employees who will be using the module, including sales representatives, customer service representatives, and finance personnel. By providing comprehensive user training, businesses can ensure that the implementation is successful and that the employees are able to use the module efficiently and effectively.

Manage Change Effectively

Change management is an important consideration in SAP SD implementation. The implementation may require changes to business processes, job roles, and responsibilities. By managing change effectively, businesses can ensure that the implementation is successful and that employees are able to adapt to the new system. Change management should include communication, engagement, and incentives for using the new system.

Perform Thorough Testing

Thorough testing is critical for ensuring that the SAP SD module is functioning correctly and that there are no issues or bugs in the system. Testing should include unit testing, integration testing, and user acceptance testing. By performing thorough testing, businesses can identify and address any issues before they become major problems.

Monitor and Evaluate Performance

Once the SAP SD module has been implemented, it is important to monitor and evaluate performance. This involves tracking key performance indicators (KPIs) and analyzing data to identify areas for improvement. By monitoring and evaluating performance, businesses can identify areas for improvement and take action to improve the overall efficiency and quality of the sales and distribution process.

Conclusion

Implementing the SAP SD module is a significant undertaking for any business. By following these best practices and tips for successful implementation, businesses can ensure that the implementation is successful and that the module is configured to meet their specific needs. Successful SAP SD implementation can help businesses improve their sales and distribution process, increase efficiency, and reduce costs.

Printed in Great Britain
by Amazon

26217655R00024